I WISH I HAD MY FATHER

NORMA SIMON pictures by Arieh Zeldich

ALBERT WHITMAN & COMPANY, NILES, ILLINOIS

For the wise young Wellfleet children
who helped me write this book

Library of Congress Cataloging in Publication Data

Simon, Norma.
    I wish I had my father.

    Summary: Father's Day is tough for a boy whose
father left him years ago and never communicates
with him.
    [1. Fathers and sons—Fiction] I. Zeldich, Arieh,
1949– . II. Title.
PZ7.S6053Iah 1983   [E]   83-1287
ISBN 0-8075-3522-2 (lib. bdg.)

A Note About This Book

There are today many boys and girls who live with one parent and visit their other parent. But the children in this book live in a single parent family and do not see or know the parent who doesn't live with them.

Discussions with children about their thoughts and feelings concerning their distant, unknown parents resulted in *I Wish I Had My Father*. The cheerful, resilient children who talked about this delicate subject have learned to cope with their less-than-perfect life situations. They seemed to welcome an opportunity to explore their conflicting emotions and to discover that other children are in similar situations. Caring single parents help these children accept themselves and become aware of the great variety of life styles and families that exist around them.

Adult understanding and appreciation can ease some of the painful rejection felt by children like the narrator of the story and his friend Grace. This book can begin to help adults and children find words to express the thoughts, memories, emotions, and expectations that surround the significant, though absent, parent in the children's lives.

Norma Simon

I hate Father's Day,
and here it comes again.

Every year, in June,
before school's over,
the teacher tells us,
"We're all going to make
something for our fathers."

And every year, since nursery school,
I put my hand up.
Some of the other kids do, too.
This year the teacher calls on Grace.

"Yes, Grace?" he asks her.
"I don't have a father," Grace tells him.

"I know you have a father," the teacher says.
"Everyone has a father and a mother.
But your father doesn't live with you."

"Well, I never even see him," Grace says.
"I never see my dad, either," I say.

"You could still make something
for your fathers and mail the presents
to them," our teacher says.

"No, I can't," says Grace.
"We don't know his address."
"I don't know my dad's address, either,"
I tell the teacher.

"Well," the teacher says,
"maybe you can give
your Father's Day present
to someone else you like a lot."

I wish I didn't have to make
something for Father's Day.
I wish I had a father
I could know.

Some kids in my class
can't stand Mother's Day.
They don't know where
their mothers are living,
and they don't see them anymore.

But I like Mother's Day.
I love to give my mother a present.

If there was an Uncle's Day,
I would want to make something.

I have nice uncles.
I see them on Thanksgiving and other holidays.

If there was a Grandma and Grandpa's Day,
that would be fine with me.
I see Grandma and Grandpa once a year.
I visit them in California.

But I hate Father's Day,
and so does my friend Grace.
Grace says she wishes she had a father
who lived with her mother and brother and her.

Some of the other kids in our class
don't live with their fathers,
but they see them sometimes.
And my friend Mark's father died in an accident
when Mark was just a baby.

But my father is still alive and I never see him.
My mother tells me she thinks my father loves me.
She says he's living someplace far away.

But if he loves me, how come
he doesn't send me postcards?
or telephone me?
or come to see me?

He doesn't even know my nickname
or remember my birthday is
September twenty-fifth.

I miss him when I see
other kids with their fathers.
It feels like bumping a sore
and making it hurt again.

My friend Jeff has a nice father.
He always plays baseball with us
when I visit Jeff.
When we're eating supper at Jeff's house,
and his father makes a joke,
everyone laughs.

I wonder if my father ever makes jokes,
wherever he is.

My mother told me
that once upon a time
when they used to be married,
my mother and father loved each other,
and we were all happy together.

But that was a long time ago,
before I remember.

My mother said they began to argue
and fight and it was awful.
She told me, "Sometimes people need a divorce
when they make each other very unhappy."

She said my father even used
to yell at me, when I was a baby,
and I used to cry. That upset her, too,
and made my mom and dad
yell at each other even more.

My mother doesn't really like to talk about my father.
It makes her sad.
It makes me sad, too, when I think about him.

We don't have pictures of my father around the house.
But we have his picture in my baby book.
He looks nice. He's laughing in the picture.
I'll bet he'd laugh if he could see me
with my four front teeth out.

Maybe I'll see my dad
someday
when I grow up.

Right now I just wish Father's Day
didn't keep coming around.

I wonder how my father would have liked
all the things I've made for Father's Day.
This year my teacher says we're going to make
fancy Father's Day cards.

When I was in kindergarten,
I made a dog out of clay.
Mom said I should mail it to Grandpa.
He called me on the telephone
when he got my package.
It made me happy to talk to him.

Last year I gave the seed painting I made
to Mr. MacKnight downstairs. He takes care of me
after school until Mom gets home from work.
He's sort of like a grandpa. He taught me
how to play checkers. Sometimes I even win.
Mr. MacKnight hung the seed painting
up in his bedroom. He likes it a lot.

This year my teacher says Grace and I
don't have to make cards,
if we don't want to.

But I guess I will.

I'll make one for Grandpa,
with a picture of our dog and cat on it.
I'll make one for Mr. MacKnight,
with a picture of a checkerboard.
And I'll make one for my friend Jon,
with a picture of a big fish.
Jon loves to go fishing,
and sometimes he takes my mom and me.

I wonder if my dad would like
a card from me on Father's Day?

I wonder if he thinks of me at all?

On the way home from school, Grace and I talk.

"Don't you wish there was no Father's Day?"
Grace asks me. "That's what I wish."

"Not really," I tell her.
"If my wish could come true,
I'd have my father at least one day in the year."